DATE DUE

Historical Atlases of South Asia,
Central Asia, and the Middle East

A HISTORICAL ATLAS OF

AFGHANISTAN

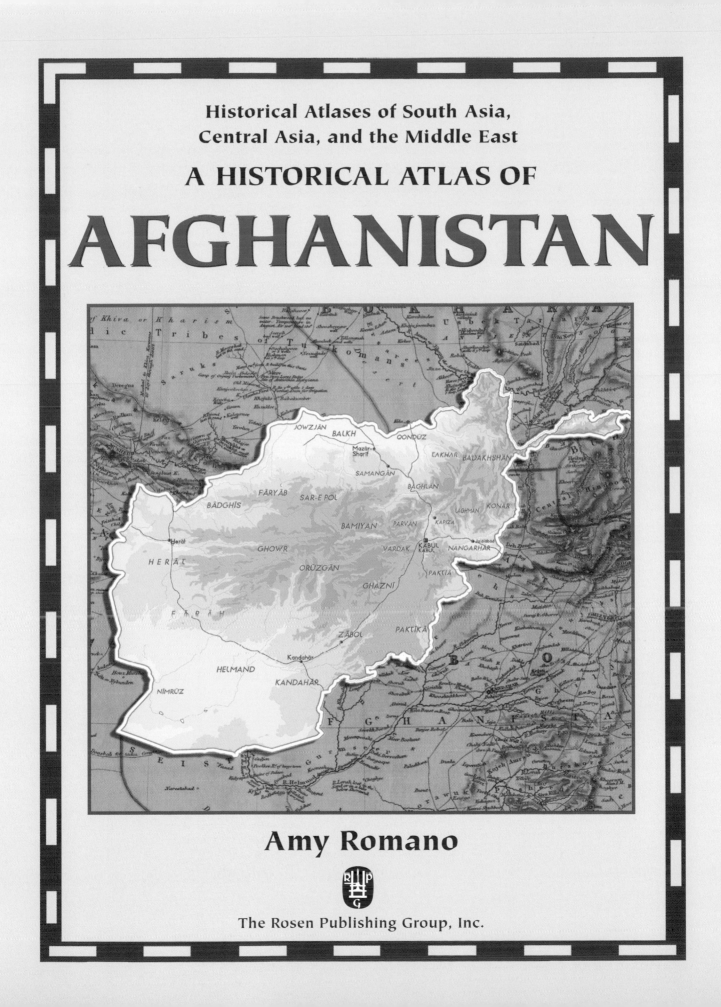

Amy Romano

The Rosen Publishing Group, Inc.

Published in 2003 by The Rosen Publishing Group, Inc.
29 East 21st Street, New York, NY 10010

Copyright © 2003 by The Rosen Publishing Group, Inc.

First Edition

Library of Congress Cataloging-in-Publication Data

Romano, Amy.
A Historical Atlas of Afghanistan / by Amy Romano. — 1st ed.
   p. cm. — (Historical atlases of South Asia, Central Asia, and the Middle East)
Includes bibliographical references and index.
Summary: Maps and text chronicle the history of Afghanistan, from the Aryan invasion in 1500 B.C. to the rise of the Taliban.
ISBN 0-8239-3863-8
1. Afghanistan—History—Maps for children. 2. Afghanistan—Maps for children.
[1. Afghanistan—History. 2. Atlases.]
I. Title. II. Series.
G2266.S1R6 2002
911'.581—dc21

                                                                    2002031034

Manufactured in the United States of America

Cover image: Afghanistan *(current/nineteenth-century maps, center)* has been overcome by conquerors as evidenced in the Mongol tile *(bottom left)*, guided by pivotal leaders such as Dost Muhammad Khan *(top left)*, and guarded by modern rebels *(right)*.

Contents

INTRODUCTION

Most people know Afghanistan only as a nation of war and ruins, but it is a country with a remarkable history. With a name that literally means "land of the Afghans," Afghanistan is a section of central Asia rich in art, architecture, and archaeology.

It wasn't until the middle of the nineteenth century (1857) that Afghanistan officially defined its borders. For centuries, the region had held historical significance because of its location—straddling trade routes between the Indian subcontinent, Iran, and central Asia. It was a territory that tempted conquerors and countries.

Today, Afghanistan shares its borders with six countries of central Asia and the Middle East. Its western border

Afghanistan—the land of the Afghans—is a landlocked country with a population of 26.8 million people. Since the 1970s, Afghanistan's government has been unstable, suffering several coups, the last one in 1978 by Afghan communists. Since that time the country has been at war, first with the Soviets and more recently with the United States. As a result, most of its cities, including its capital Kabul, lie completely in ruin. Most highways and bridges have been destroyed, and at least 4 million Afghans live as refugees.

Over the years, sections of Afghanistan have yielded archaeological evidence dating back more than 30,000 years. This photo, though not of the skull fragments found in Darra-I-Kur, Afghanistan, is a common example of a Neanderthal skull. People may have traveled the lands later known as Afghanistan as early as 100,000 BC.

eastern and southern borders—a boundary line that has been hotly disputed for centuries. Afghanistan has 3,538 miles (5,529 kilometers) of land borders and is roughly the size of the state of Texas. It is a country without seaports or harbors.

In its earliest history, Afghanistan was likely home to Paleolithic man, based on artifacts that were found in its northern territories, such as parts of a Neanderthal skull. Historians also believe it was a region where humans first began domesticating animals and plants, indicating an advanced civilization. Despite these discoveries, today Afghanistan remains one of the world's least developed countries.

Known in ancient times as Aryana, and as Khorasan in medieval times, Afghanistan has had an evolution that is both splendid and horrific. Each conquest of the region, and its transition between development and destruction, largely corresponds with the rise and fall of empires and religions.

sits against Iran. Turkmenistan, Uzbekistan, and Tajikistan make up Afghanistan's natural northernmost border, generally following the route of the Amu Darya River. At the far end of its northeastern Wakhan Corridor, Afghanistan borders China. Pakistan, formally the northwestern portion of India until 1947, frames its

1 EARLY INVADERS

Beginning as early as 1500 BC, Aryan warriors from Eurasia invaded the territory known today as Afghanistan. Heading toward India, they settled in the fertile north central plains of Bactria, present-day Balkh. Throughout history, Aryan descendants played a critical role in many of central Asia's greatest empires. As they settled into what is now Afghanistan, northern India, Iran, and Pakistan, Aryans brought with them skills that kept their empire dominant for nearly 1,000 years. They organized governments and a successful system of agriculture.

By 540 BC, Cyrus the Great, a member of the noble Achaemenid family of Persia (present day Iran), began his quest to overthrow ancient Bactria. He wanted the fertile territory as a part of his own empire. But Bactria would not come under Persian rule until 522 BC with the invasion of King Darius I, another member of the Achaemenid family. With this replacement of Aryan rule by Persian powers, so began Afghanistan's history as the pawn of central Asia.

With these reigns, now dominated by Cyrus the Great and King Darius I, the Achaemenid Empire would begin a 200-year stronghold in the region, eventually controlling central Asia. Following Darius, his son Xerxes continued expanding the empire. He ultimately extended control in a westward direction from India through central Asia to the Mediterranean Sea,

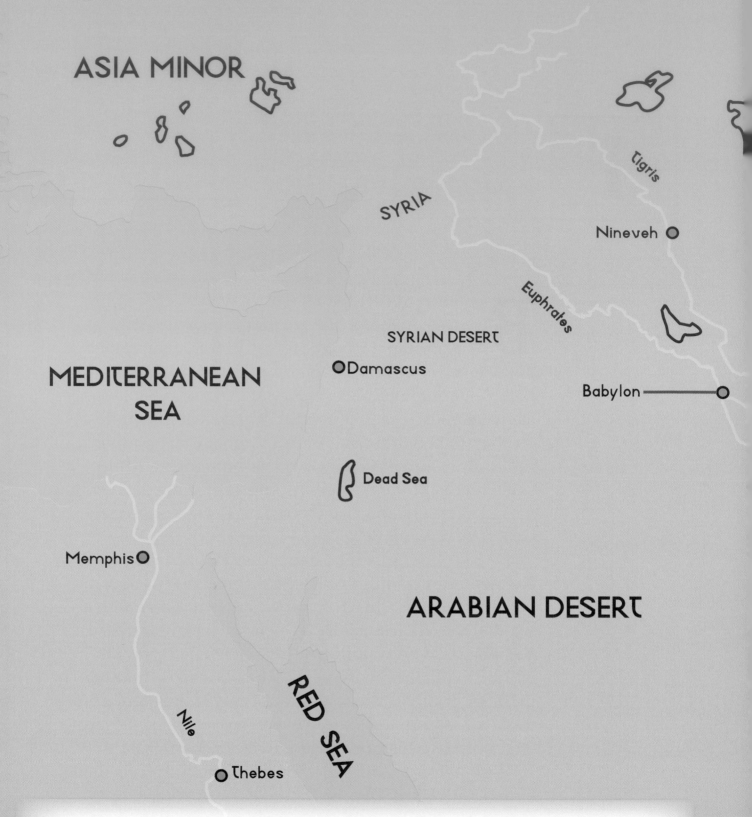

ASIA MINOR

Tigris

SYRIA

Nineveh ○

Euphrates

SYRIAN DESERT

○ Damascus

Babylon ──────○

MEDITERRANEAN
SEA

Dead Sea

Memphis ○

ARABIAN DESERT

RED SEA

Nile

○ Thebes

Darius the Great, one of the original rulers of the Achaemenid Empire from 522 to 486 BC, is remembered most for dividing the Persian territories into separate states, or satrapies. Darius was considered a successful leader in his day—a diplomat who kept the region peaceful while expanding Persian territories. He had remarkable structures and roadways built both during and after his reign, and he established cities in Susa and Persepolis. His son Xerxes, seen here in the Portico of Xerxes *(top right)*, was king of the Achaemenid Empire from 485 to 465 BC. Persepolis (in present-day Iran), where this relief sculpture was found, was once the city of residence for all Persian kings.

CASPIAN SEA

O Susa

Persepolis O

Persian Gulf

including Egypt. This expansion created the largest empire of the ancient world. With Xerxes' advances, the conquered regions of central Asia experienced the development of a governing system and a network of roads, as well as one of the world's first major religions, Zoroastrianism. Now rare, Zoroastrianism later became known as Parsee (or Parsis). It is still practiced in India and Iran. After Xerxes' death in 465 BC, the power of the Achaemenid Empire began to decline.

Greek Rule

While the Achaemenid Empire was advancing from Persia, the Macedonian Empire, in what is now southeastern Europe, was expanding. In control was a young Macedonian king named Alexander the Great who had assumed the throne of Macedonia after the death of his father in 336 BC. Based on the shores of the Aegean Sea, the empire extended north through present-day Yugoslavia and Bulgaria and south to Greece. Soon Macedonian armies began expeditions throughout Asia toward India. Macedonian soldiers wanted to reach the Ganges River and the Indian Ocean, increasing the empire's wealth through improved trade routes and relationships. Alexander then began his conquest of the Achaemenid Empire.

Alexander's goals were to control the known world and colonize its unknown territories. Each of his conquests united Greek and Asian cultures. Greek became the common language in Alexander's empire, and both Macedonians and Persians ruled as satraps, or governors of provinces.

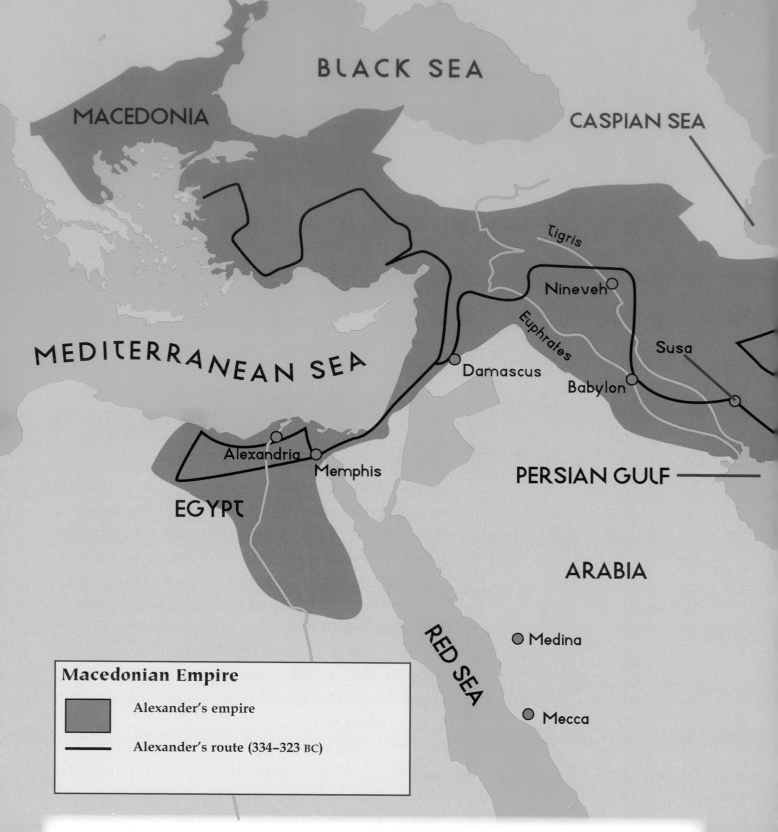

BLACK SEA

MACEDONIA

CASPIAN SEA

Tigris

Nineveh

MEDITERRANEAN SEA

Euphrates

Susa

Damascus

Babylon

PERSIAN GULF

Alexandria

Memphis

EGYPT

ARABIA

Medina

RED SEA

Mecca

Macedonian Empire

Alexander's empire

Alexander's route (334–323 BC)

Alexander the Great (356–323 BC), son of Philip II of Macedonia, invaded the Persian Empire in 331 BC and founded colonies in present-day Afghanistan before heading south into India. His Macedonian Empire, as it was known, was spread too far and too wide, however, and after Alexander's unexpected death in 323 BC his vast territories were split among his generals, the most important of whom was Seleucus, founder of the Seleucid dynasty.

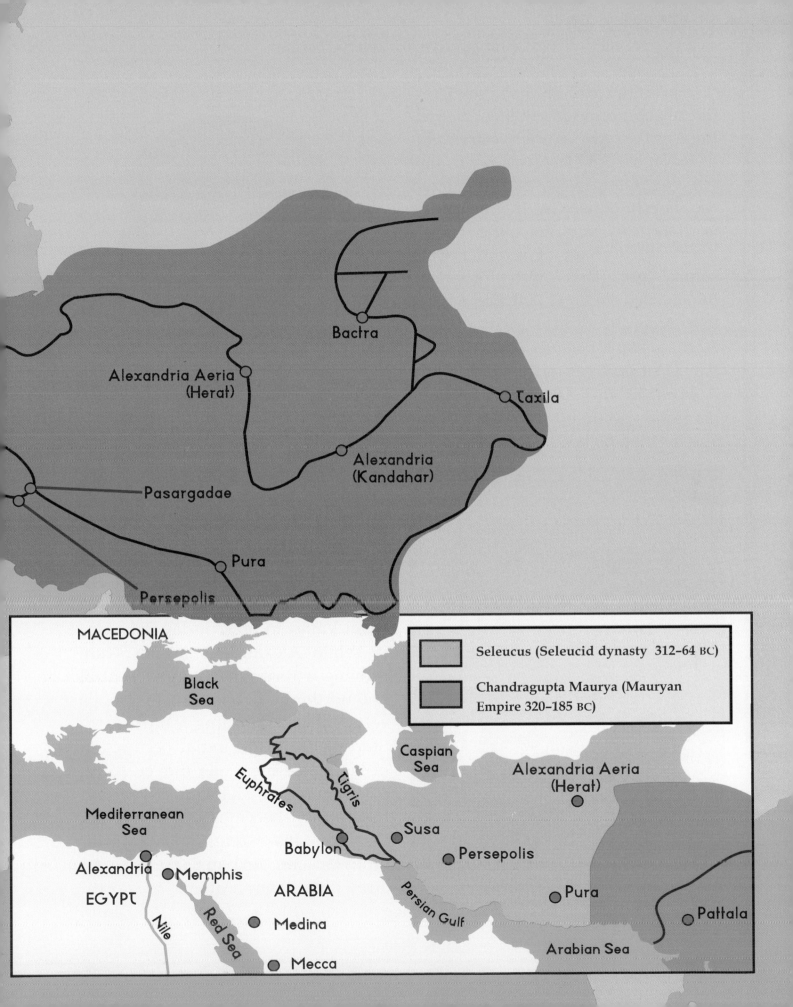

Bactra

Alexandria Aeria
(Herat)

Taxila

Alexandria
(Kandahar)

Pasargadae

Pura

Persepolis

MACEDONIA

Black
Sea

Caspian
Sea

Alexandria Aeria
(Herat)

Euphrates

Tigris

Mediterranean
Sea

Susa

Babylon

Alexandria

Persepolis

Memphis

EGYPT

ARABIA

Pura

Persian Gulf

Pattala

Nile

Red Sea

Medina

Arabian Sea

Mecca

Seleucus (Seleucid dynasty 312–64 BC)

Chandragupta Maurya (Mauryan
Empire 320–185 BC)

Alexander and his armies entered the Afghan region in 330 BC, defeating the Persians in the western city of Herat on the Hari Rud River. Just one year later, in 329 BC, he entered the Hindu Kush in the country's northeastern territory. The Hindu Kush are a chain of mountains in central Asia that stretch approximately 600 miles (1,000 kilometers) between the Indus River near Afghanistan's eastern border to the Amu Darya River in the north.

From 328 to 327 BC, Alexander and his troops occupied the Hindu Kush and the land on both sides of the Amu

This bust of a deity, found in Takht-e Kobad, Turkistan, is an Achaemenid sculpture that dates from the fifth century BC. Now located in London's British Museum, scholars theorize that it could be portraying Alexander the Great.

Darya. He made one final move in 326 that extended Macedonian territory to the upper region of the Indus River Valley in present-day Pakistan.

While Alexander's armies were moving across what is now central and northern Afghanistan, his troops were also extending southward. Starting from the initial occupation of Herat, his men later moved south to Sistan on the Helmand River, and then established a city in Kandahar. During his reign, Alexander amassed an expansive territory stretching from Athens to northwestern India (now Pakistan).

This detail of an ancient floor mosaic illustrates the Battle of Issus in 333 BC between Alexander the Great and Persian armies under the leadership of Darius III. The mosaic was created in the first century BC in Naples, Italy.

Alexander the Great secured his place as one of history's most powerful generals.

Alexander's empire, now crumbling after his death, was divided among his commanders into city-states. In south Asia, Seleucus, a former general, founded the Seleucid dynasty. Seleucid territories included the northwestern province of Bactria and the former Persian provinces north and east of the Hindu Kush. For seven decades, until about 64 BC, the Seleucids founded many cities.

At the same time, the land south of the Hindu Kush was conquered by Chandragupta Maurya, founder of the Mauryan dynasty.

The Mauryan dynasty was the first empire that organized a unified government in the region and imposed a system of taxation. Trade increased because a system of weights and measures became standardized. Public irrigation systems were developed, which helped produce bountiful harvests. People worked as artisans making cloth, jewelry, and wooden products, or farmed

Afghanistan's Hindu Kush mountains—a name that literally means "Hindu killer"—were most likely given their name because of the region's harsh lifestyle and the difficulties the mountains represented for outside invaders. They are located at the western end of the Himalaya Mountains, and are usually covered with snow from November to March. Few people can pass through the mountains during the winter, and when they do, it is most often by horseback. The only modern pass through the Hindu Kush was a tunnel built by the Soviets during their occupation of Afghanistan in the 1980s that links Kabul to the former Soviet border.

the land. Additionally, one of Chandragupta's successors, Asoka, became responsible not only for maintaining Mauryan control, but also for

The Mauryan Empire (320–185 BC), founded by Chandragupta Maurya, encompassed what is now present-day Afghanistan as well as most of India. This sculpture, which dates from that period, is of a crocodile, or *makara*, a common figure in Hindu mythology.

establishing Buddhism in the region, building religious centers in and south of the Hindu Kush. Stupas, or shrines that housed Buddhist sculptures and artifacts, were erected. Afghanistan's most famous Buddhist site is in Bamiyan where two giant Buddhas once stood. Although divided, what was once a Macedonian empire, ruled by Alexander the Great, remained predominantly Greek until the middle of the second century AD.

2 THE RISE OF RELIGION

As a result of travel and trade between India, China, and the central Asian kingdoms, the land that is now Afghanistan developed both religiously and artistically. Buddhism and Islam played critical roles in the region's progress, and alliances and rivalries impacted an area most Westerners now refer to as the Middle East.

The Kushans

After the fall of Alexander the Great and the Macedonian Empire, a series of invasions and short-lived dynasties marked the approximate period from 350 to 150 BC. Minor occupations by the nomadic Scythians, invaders from other parts of central Asia, as well as the Parthians, a people who only temporarily regained independence from the Persian and Seleucid Empires, occurred before the Kushans took hold.

Originally from northwestern China, the Kushans ruled the region by the late second century BC. By the middle of the first century AD, they established a capital in Peshawar, now located in Pakistan. The Kushans also ruled Gandhara, an area now known as the Kabul Valley. This gave them control from the lower Indus River to the modern Iranian border, and from the Chinese province of Sinkiang Xinjiang, to the Caspian and Arabian Seas.

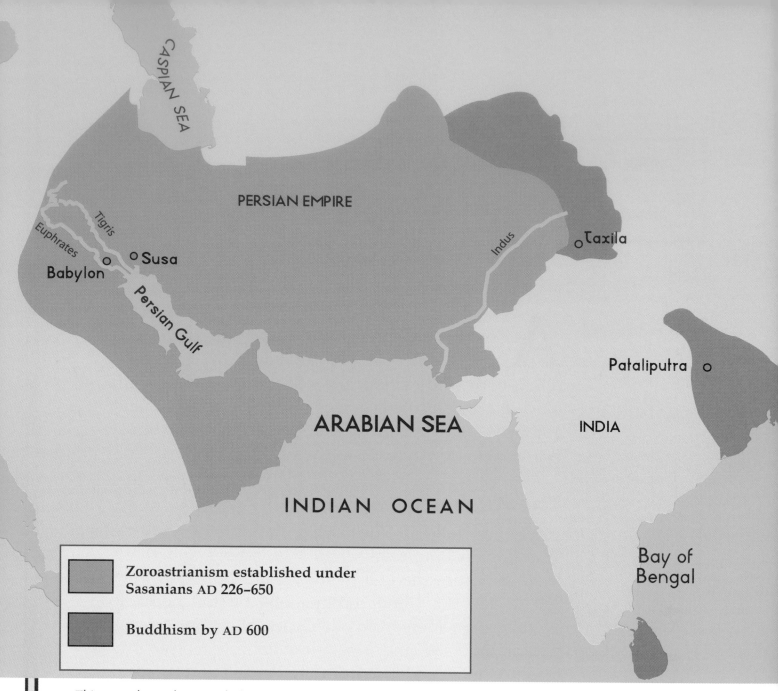

This map shows the spread of Zoroastrianism, the faith of the Persian kings, and of Buddhism, a religion begun by Siddhartha Gautama (*map inset*), later known as Buddha, or "the enlightened one." Buddhism spread as far east as China over the course of about 200 years. The Bamiyan Buddha (*bottom right*), in central Afghanistan, was among several 2,000-year-old sculptures that were destroyed by fundamentalist Taliban forces in 2001 because they were considered an insult to Islam. Before its destruction, this sculpture was the world's tallest standing Buddha at 175 feet (53 meters).

During the Kushan dynasty, which lasted until the early third century AD, Buddhism, the official religion of the Kushans, became the dominant influence in Gandhara. In an effort to gain popularity, King Kanishka called a council of Buddhist scholars in Kashmir (a state now divided between India and Pakistan), and decided to reinterpret

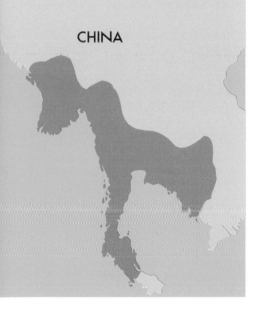

CHINA

Buddhism. With this council, a new school of Buddhism called Mahayana was developed. Mahayana Buddhism would later spread to the Far East and parts of Southeast Asia. Its creation sparked the first representation of Buddha in an artistic form.

The attraction of Buddhist art grew. The most famous site is located in Afghanistan, in the central province of Bamiyan. Although scarred by centuries of war, two colossal Buddha statues carved out of rock more than 1,600 years ago once stood nearly 180 feet (55 meters) high until they were both destroyed by Afghan militants in 2001.

In addition to bringing a unified religious base to the region, the Kushans also protected and promoted trade along the Silk Road, a 5,000-mile (8,047-kilometer) route that linked India and China with the Mediterranean Sea. Under the direction of King Kanishka, the largest trade of goods was transported through Balkh, a major exchange center located in what is now Afghanistan. Deriving its name from the incredible amount of Chinese silk and other luxury items that were transported along it, the Silk Road made trading in the region accessible

and profitable. Afghanistan's rich deposits of lapis lazuli (a blue semi-precious stone) secured its position as a point of commerce along this historic route.

In the middle of the third century, the Kushan dynasty crumbled. Persian tribes from the northern mountains took advantage of the fragmented empire and seized control of the region. Now calling themselves Sassanians, these former Persians enjoyed relatively undisturbed dominance over both the Persian and Kushan Empires for more than four centuries. The Sassanian Empire included modern Afghanistan and Pakistan territories west of the Indus River.

The Birth of Islam

The Sassanian Empire reached its height in the middle of the sixth century after overcoming Roman forces. These conflicts stemmed from religious differences. The Romans adopted Christianity in the fourth century, and the Sassanians remained loyal to Zoroastrian teachings. Sassanian forces expanded their empire as far as Constantinople (present-day Istanbul, Turkey). Unfortunately, after a short-lived victory, they were defeated by Arab armies in 642 and lost physical and religious control of the region.

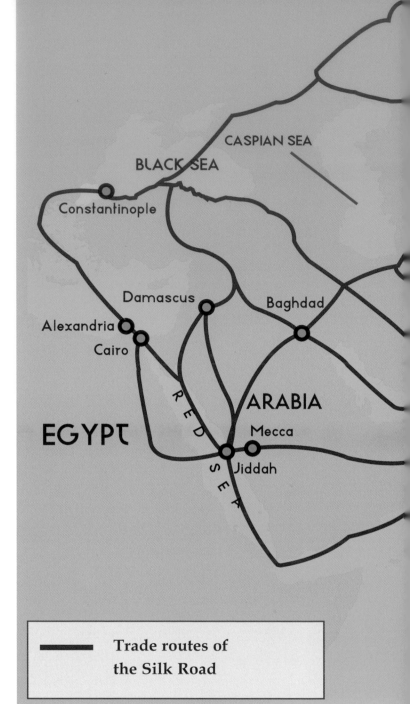

Trade routes of the Silk Road

Muhammad, the Islamic prophet, died in 632. Afterward, Arab rulers spread his religious teachings. Islamic forces began moving into the region that is now known as Afghanistan. In many ways, the Islamic conquest of Afghanistan that began in the

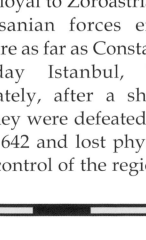

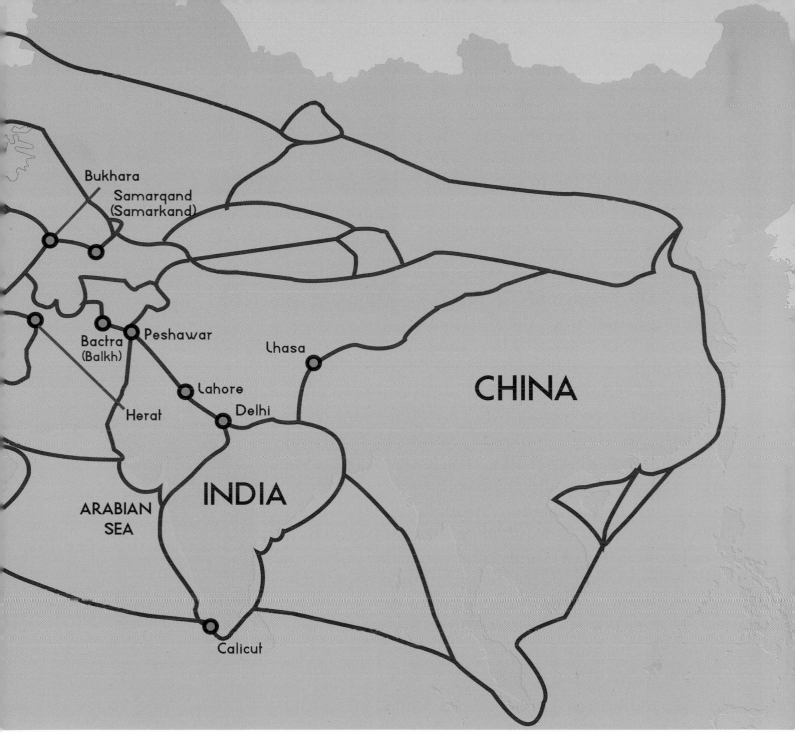

Bukhara
Samarqand
(Samarkand)

Bactra
(Balkh)
Peshawar
Lhasa
Herat
Lahore
Delhi

CHINA

INDIA

ARABIAN
SEA

Calicut

The Silk Road—a 5,000-mile (8,047-km) trade route over land and sea—linked scores of merchants between Europe and China from 100 BC. Over the years, the famous road fell into disuse, however, beginning with the conquests of the Mongols. It regained some popularity during the thirteenth century AD, but was closed for good in 1453 when Muslim Ottomans (Turks) forbade European Christians from traveling its stretches, and Europeans discovered longer trade routes across the seas.

middle of the seventeenth century continues today. This period of Islamic influence entrenched itself in the region for centuries to come.

Arab armies centered in Persia (Iran) mounted an expedition in 652. Now the western city of Herat and the southwestern center of Sistan

Alexandria ○

would come under Islamic rule. By 667, Kabul was also a center of Islamic power, and by 714, the Arab empire extended throughout the entire region, up to and including the Indus River.

Arab control of the region remained strong until 920. It was around that time that Muslim rulers called Samanids, a people who originated from the Bukhara province in what is now Uzbekistan, exerted their power. The Samanids' influence extended south across the Amu Darya River and into present-day Afghanistan. With this advance, an Islamic empire that stretched from India to Baghdad was born. Balkh, the center of commerce and Buddhism for the Kushan Empire, had been converted to an Islamic stronghold. Although Islam was about to experience explosive growth, it would not last. Just twenty years after their advance, the Samanids would face the end of their reign in the region. Former Turkish slaves from the northwest defied their Persian masters and took control.

The Ghaznavid Dynasty

By 962, the former Turkish slaves gained significant influence over their masters. One slave in particular, Abu Mansur Sebüktigin, married the daughter of Sultan Mahmud of Ghazni. The sultan was a leader who ruled the ancient city of Ghazni and developed the mountainous area. Upon the governor's death,

The Ghazni Minaret, one of the only remains of the Ghaznavid dynasty, was once covered in blue stones called lapis lazuli. Ghazni was once the capital of Afghanistan where historians, poets, and scientists often gathered to form a royal court, led by one ruling family.

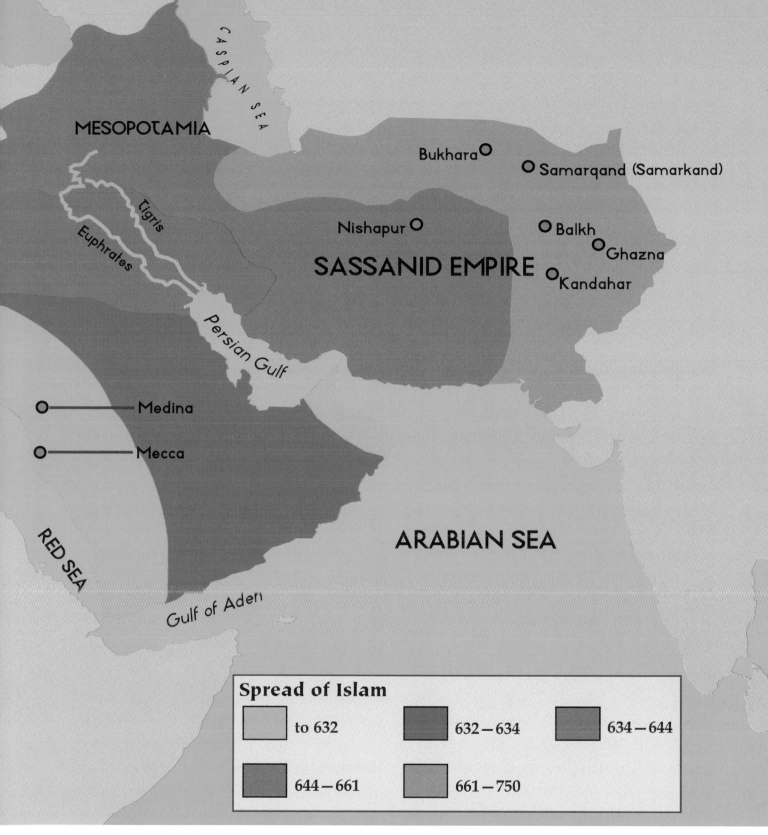

Spread of Islam

to 632	632–634	634–644
644–661	661–750	

Islam, the faith practiced by Muslims and a name that literally means "submission to God," spread rapidly after its founder, Muhammad (AD 570–632) died. The religion gained converts first in present-day Saudi Arabia and then moved south to present-day Yemen and north to Syria. By AD 750, Islam spread as far west as Spain. Afghanistan had officially converted to Islam by AD 709.

Islam

Islam is the name given to the religion preached by the prophet Muhammad beginning in AD 600. The world's second-largest religion after Christianity, Islam is based on the concept of *tawheed*, the oneness of God, and the belief that Muhammad is the last in a long line of prophets including Abraham, Moses, and Jesus.

After Muhammad's death, Muslims (practitioners of Islam) divided into two sects. People who believed that Muhammad's successor, the caliph (community leader), should be elected ruler became known as the Sunni. Others who believed that only Muhammad's blood descendants could rule became known as the Shia. The majority of Muslims in the world are Sunni. Most conservative or fundamentalist Muslims are Sunni and follow a strict interpretation of Islam. Members of the Shia group are called Shiites. Iran is the only Shia majority state.

Sebüktigin became the governor himself and immediately declared independence from the Samanids. He set about establishing his own kingdom that his son Mahmud greatly expanded, looting wealth from India.

Thirty years into Ghaznavid rule, Mahmud of Ghazni, who ruled from 998 to 1030, combined the various conquests of his predecessors and centered the region's capital in the city of Ghazni, which is now situated in east-central Afghanistan, about 70 miles (113 kilometers) south of Kabul. Having a great fondness for art, Mahmud is credited with developing the region into a cultural and educational center, rich with beautiful architecture. He also used Ghazni as a base for conquests into India.

Mahmud was in power for thirty-two years and was considered one of the greatest of Afghanistan's ancient leaders. For nearly 200 years, the Ghaznavid dynasty, weakening with each successive leader, contributed to the expansion of Islam within the region and into India. Although many of Mahmud's palaces have been destroyed, there are two twelfth-century minarets that still stand on the outskirts of Ghazni. A great arch and citadel at Bost (Lashkar Gah) also remain as a testament to the once sophisticated empire.

3 DEVASTATION AND REBIRTH

The Ghaznavid dynasty grew weaker through the twelfth century, finally giving way in 1186 to a new period of conquest. The invasions devastated the landscape and more than 1,000 years of consistent progress.

In the early thirteenth century, a new dynasty would mercilessly sweep across the region. Led by Genghis Khan, chieftain of the Mongols who invaded Afghanistan from Mongolia, the invasion and occupation lasted from 1219 until 1223. It resulted in the destruction of many cities in Asia, mostly north of the Gobi Desert. Irrigation systems, vital to the growth of agriculture that had developed over the past millennium, also came under attack.

Invasion of the Mongols

Genghis Khan was likely born between 1162 and 1167 to a local chieftain of the Mongol tribe near the present-day border between Mongolia and southeastern Russia. Named Temüjin at birth, he would come to be known as Chinggis-Khan (Genghis Khan). Shortly before Genghis Khan's conquest of present-day Afghanistan, Mongol leaders acclaimed him their supreme leader. Loosely translated, Genghis Khan means "universal monarch," a title that would not be lost on Genghis Khan. As a direct result of his military

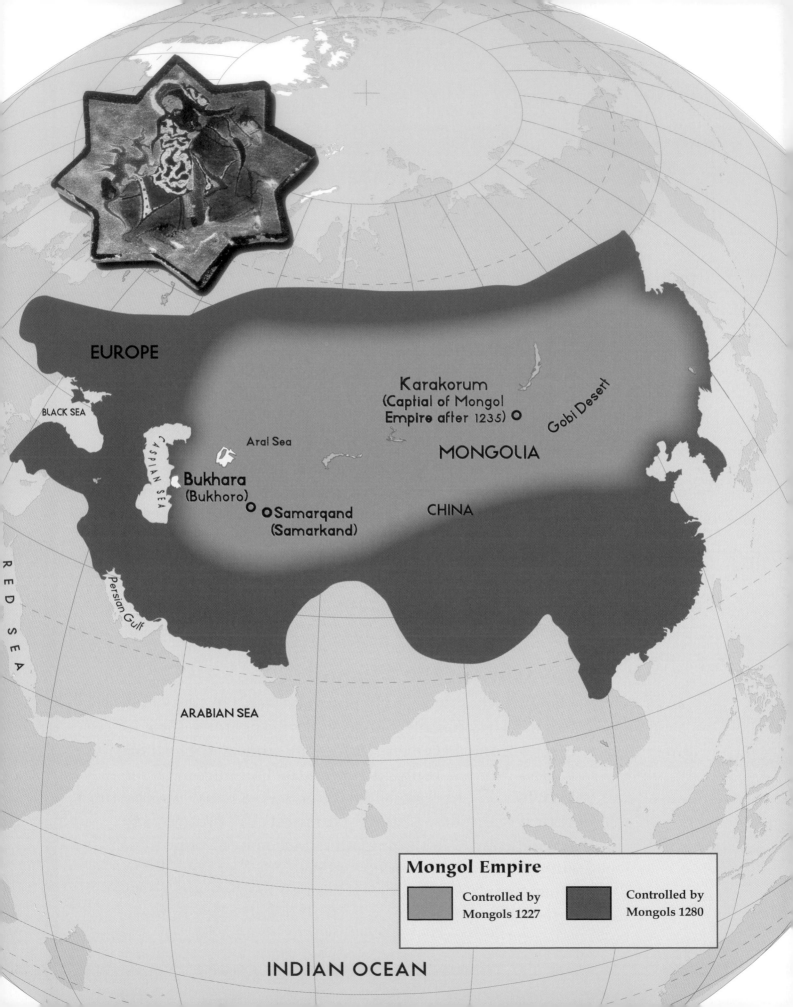

EUROPE

BLACK SEA

CASPIAN SEA

Aral Sea

Karakorum
(Captial of Mongol
Empire after 1235) O

Gobi Desert

MONGOLIA

Bukhara
(Bukhoro) O

O Samarqand
(Samarkand)

CHINA

RED SEA

Persian Gulf

ARABIAN SEA

INDIAN OCEAN

Mongol Empire

Controlled by
Mongols 1227

Controlled by
Mongols 1280

genius and the conquests of his Mongol forces, Genghis Khan's Mongol Empire spanned the entire Asian continent by the time of his death in 1227.

During his four-year reign in the region, Genghis Khan reduced its prominent cities—Herat, Ghazni, Bamiyan, and Balkh—to rubble and killed thousands of people. Many historians still consider the effects in the region devastating. The cities, along with other commercial centers, shrines, monuments, crops, and irrigation systems, were systematically destroyed. Additionally, Genghis Khan's regional destruction all but eliminated the presence of Buddhism. Today virtually all of Afghanistan's twenty-seven million inhabitants are followers of Islam. Eighty-four percent follow Sunni Muslim teachings, while 15 percent are Shia Muslims.

This page from an Arabic manuscript dating from 1397–1398 shows Genghis Khan in a pulpit of a mosque in Bukhara. It now resides in England at London's British Library.

Following Genghis Khan's death, the region was slowly rebuilt. A series of his chieftains struggled for supremacy, but a true ruler would not emerge for more than 100 years.

Mongol invasions from the thirteenth century dominated the region later known as Afghanistan, killing thousands. Mongol armies nearing 200,000 soldiers devastated Herat and Bamiyan in 1221 after the khan's grandson was killed during battle. Nearby ruins in Bamiyan are known as Shahr-i-Gholghola, or the "City of Noise"—a reference that reflected the cries of dying victims. After the invasions, Afghanistan would be divided into independent sections under Mongol rule, starting with Kublai Khan, the grandson of Genghis Khan.

This page from an Arabic manuscript, another now housed at the British Library in London, shows the fourteenth-century Mongol conqueror Timur (Tamerlane) as he sits inside a towering minaret. Like conquerors before him, Timur is said to have ordered thousands killed in the region of Afghanistan, which he had seized by 1369. Legend has it that he spared the lives of known artists, most of whom he sent north to Samarkand and Bukhara to build beautiful works of architecture.

The Great Timurid Era

In 1369, a descendent of Genghis Khan named Timur, also known as Tamerlane, began incorporating present-day Afghanistan into his already vast Asian empire. His forces captured and destroyed Balkh. By 1381, he had moved into Herat, ultimately proclaiming himself emperor of a territory that stretched from Kabul to his hometown of Samarkand (in present-day Uzbekistan) and the Aral Sea. Timur's forces caused a ruination that is still evident in the wasteland of Afghanistan's Helmand Valley.

Despite the destruction he routinely ordered, Timur had a humane side to his personality. His fondness for the arts, specifically sculpture and poetry, led to one of the richest periods in Afghan history. The Great Timurid Era, as it is known, was a time when Timur and his descendents promoted education, architecture, painting, and commerce. This century of prosperity helped each city reach its zenith. Shrines, mosques, and *madrasas* (religious schools) were built. The city of Herat became an arts center and home to the greatest Islamic talents of the time, including Kamal ad-Din Bihzad, and poets Jami and Alisher Navoi.

The Great Timurid Era began to decline in 1504 when a new invader, Zuhir-ud-Din Muhammad Babur, entered the region and captured Kabul. By 1522, Babur held power in Herat and Kandahar. He assumed control of the region into his Mughal Empire. Under Babur, Afghanistan reached the height of its military power.

Babur was a descendent of Genghis Khan on his mother's side and of Timur on his father's. He began his own exploits in Afghanistan at twenty-one years of age after losing control of his kingdom in Ferghana, an area located east of Samarkand in present-day Uzbekistan. A man of compassion as well as a great conqueror, Babur did not allow his troops to plunder goods or harm innocent people. He was also a nature lover and poet and was known as the Prince of Gardeners.

After failing for decades to recapture his homeland, Babur turned his attention to India. Using his Afghan base to regularly invade India, he left Kabul in 1526 and settled into a new Indian capital named Agra, founding the Mughal dynasty. As a result, his seat of power in

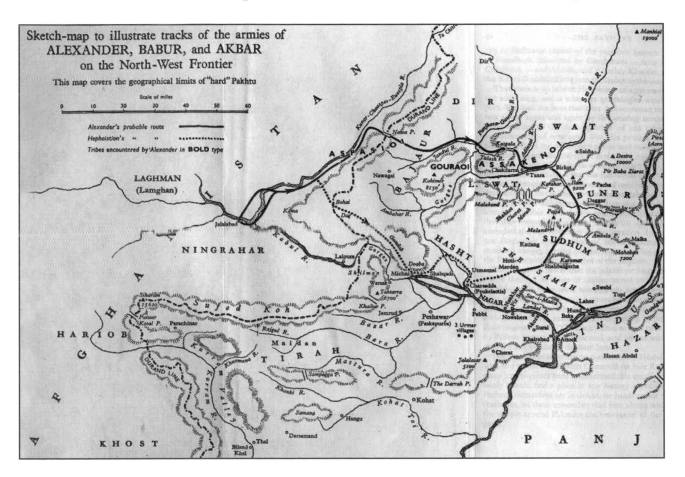

This historic map shows the routes traveled by Macedonian leader Alexander the Great, and the Mughal emperors Akbar the Great and his grandfather Babur during the sixteenth and seventeenth centuries. Babur, whose name literally means "the Tiger," is often remembered for being a great and compassionate leader who fought alongside his men. In 1504, he captured Kabul, Afghanistan, beginning what would later be known as the Mughal Empire, spanning thousands of miles eastward into India.

Afghanistan was now merely an adjacent principality. Eastern Afghanistan to the Hindu Kush, however, remained a part of Babur's territory. With his death in 1530, present-day Afghanistan was a valuable land. It became a pawn in the battle between the Mughals of India and the Safavids of Persia, a people who already controlled the western part of the territory.

For the next two centuries, boundaries in present-day Afghanistan changed. Cities, particularly Kandahar, changed hands frequently. Although India's Mughals and Iran's Safavids were now considered the rulers of the region, nearly 350 separate tribes held power in the countryside. Ultimately, an ethnic group known as Pashtuns, whose tribes in the 1500s to the 1700s were centered in the borderlands between present-day Afghanistan and Pakistan, would emerge in power. Critical players in Afghanistan's evolving history, today Pashtuns comprise nearly 40 percent of the country's total population.

Pashtuns were largely responsible for bringing about Afghanistan's eventual independence. They helped defeat both the Mughals and Persians, as well as spearheaded Afghan triumphs in the wars against the British beginning in the 1800s. Pashtuns founded the group of Islamic rebels later known as the Taliban in 1996.

Besides his status as a renowned warrior, Babur was also known as a nature enthusiast. He carefully planted at least ten different gardens in Kabul, several of which, he wrote, "were in the height of their beauty" during the summer of 1519. In this sixteenth-century Arabic manuscript, now housed in the British Library, Babur is seen among his subjects.

THE CREATION OF A COUNTRY

For Afghanistan, the eighteenth century provided the backdrop for the emergence of powerful Pashtun tribes. It also marked a division within the Islamic religion that became its foundation. Finally, after centuries of destruction, Afghanistan became a governed nation.

Pashtuns Rise to Power

In the early 1700s, Pashtun forces took control of Afghanistan. After years of strategically pitting Mughal and Persian powers against each other, Pashtun tribes began a forty-year quest to gain control of, and independence for, the Afghan region.

In 1709, Mir Wais Khan Hotaki, a Pashtun of the Ghilzai tribe from outside the city of Kandahar, waged a successful uprising that defeated Persian forces there, which were Shiite. The freedom gained for his tribe represented the first steps toward a Pashtun Sunni revolution. Hotaki's political platform for the coup, or uprising, reflected an important ideology. It represented a division among the Afghan and Muslim people and one that separated the beliefs of all Muslims. This division would be the foundation for strife between the Afghan people and their neighbors for centuries to come.

Just thirty years after Hotaki liberated Kandahar, his successors were overthrown. A Turkic warrior, Nadir

formal name Nadir Shah. After subsequent conquests of Kandahar, Kabul, and Ghazni, Nadir Shah moved his forces into India. He defeated the Mughals in 1739 in the city of Delhi and stole the famed Peacock Throne later used by the shahs of Iran. Although Nadir Shah would continue his conquests in India and present-day Uzbekistan, his reign was shortened by his assassination. In less than ten years, a Pashtun named Ahmad Khan Abdali Durrani was crowned shah of Afghanistan and controlled the last true Afghan empire.

This fifteenth-century historic map of the Mughal Empire illustrates the estates of the great Mughal emperors including Babur, his son and successor Humayun, and Humayun's son and successor, Akbar the Great. The Mughal dynasties lasted more than 300 years (1526–1858), during which time they held territory in present-day Pakistan, India, and Afghanistan.

The Durrani Dynasty

In 1747, Ahmad Shah Durrani established his leadership by spending the next twenty-six years creating a single, larger Afghanistan. Ahmad Shah won the respect and unified support of many of Afghanistan's tribal leaders who had, up until this time, been firmly independent. From his capital in Kandahar, he also

Quli, from Khorasan, a section of present-day Iran, headed the conflict. Nadir was the leader of a band of outlaws who assumed control of the Persian Empire after six years of conquest. He was elected shah (supreme ruler) of Iran in 1736 and took the

Nadir Quli *(left)*, known as Nadir Shah after he became shah of Iran in 1736, occupied Afghan cities including Kandahar, Kabul, and Ghazni before he and his forces invaded Mughal India in 1739. Once there, his forces sacked Delhi and Lahore and looted treasures from across northern India, including the Koh-i-noor diamond and the famed Peacock Throne *(right)*. Built under the reign of Shah Jahan, also the emperor who built the Taj Mahal, the throne is gloriously decorative, embedded with precious stones set in gold.

extended the country's borders from Delhi and the Amu Darya River to the Arabian Sea. It wasn't long after his ascent to power that he was ruling the second largest Muslim empire of the time, surpassed only by the Ottoman Empire in present-day Turkey, sections of Europe, and Asia. He later became known as Ahmad Shah Baba, the "Father of Afghanistan."

Ahmad Shah died in 1772. His son, Timur Shah, would rule until his death in 1793. Timur's years as shah would be best remembered for successfully putting down rebellions and relocating Afghanistan's capital from Kandahar to Kabul where it remains today.

In 1818, the Durrani reign in Afghanistan ended. No clear ruler would emerge for more than a decade as civil war raged among rival Pashtun tribes.

International Relationships

The civil war ended in 1826 when Dost Muhammad Khan gained

control and proclaimed himself emir (prince) of Afghanistan. Muhammad Khan was the son of a Mohammadzai chieftain murdered by the Durranis. To avenge his father's death, Dost Muhammad Khan defeated the Durrani leader and brought a formal end to a decade of Afghan infighting. Unfortunately, very little of the massive Durrani Empire remained when Muhammad Khan came to power, and none of the existing borders were considered official or legal.

Afghanistan's independence soon became an international issue. Both British and Russian forces began a battle for influence in the region that continued for more than 100 years.

Because the Russian Empire wanted an outlet to the Indian Ocean, it began aggressive expansion into the region. Meanwhile, Britain wanted to protect its territory in India, an empire it felt was threatened by Russian expansion. The skirmishes caused by the Anglo-Russian rivalry would become known as the Great Game, and the bloodshed caused by conflicts between the three countries

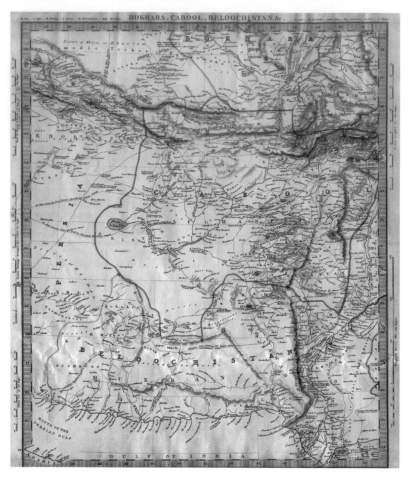

This historic map from 1838 shows the region of Bokhara (Bukhara), Caltool (Kabul), and Beloochistan (Baluchistan) as well as hours of travel by caravan over known routes. Bukhara is now a part of present-day Uzbekistan, Kabul is the current capital of Afghanistan, and Baluchistan is a province of present-day Pakistan.

continued until the early part of the twentieth century.

The Anglo-Afghan Wars

The first of three Anglo-Afghan Wars began in 1839 as Russian and British forces moved into Afghanistan. The British in India were moving toward Afghanistan from the southwest, while the Russians were advancing down from the north. When only the land in the Hindu Kush remained,

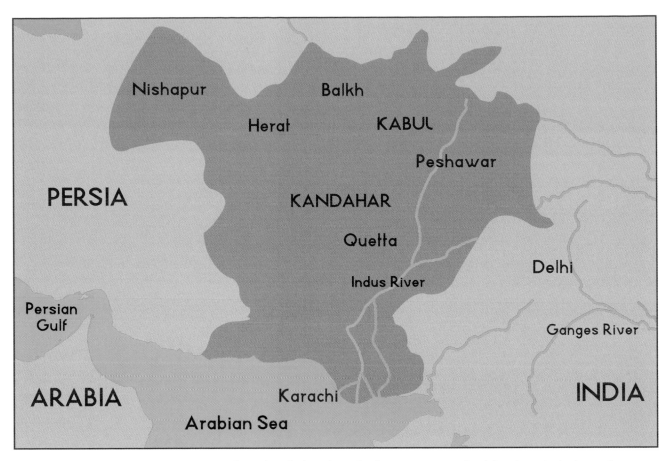

In 1747, after the assassination of Nadir Shah, Ahmad Khan announced Afghanistan's independence, founding the Durrani dynasty that same year. Under his leadership, Afghan territory reached its height, extending into present-day India before it broke apart in 1818. Later, before gradually ceding to the British Empire in India, King Amanullah Khan fought against British invaders in Afghanistan who captured Kandahar and Ghazni in 1839.

Afghanistan became the center of a struggle for control of the region.

After capturing Kandahar and Ghazni in 1839, the British temporarily gained control of Kabul and installed a puppet regime (false government) under Shah Shuja. Shah Shuja replaced Emir Dost Muhammad, who fled after his loss of power. He would regain control, however, in 1842, when Afghan rebellions against British rule finally prevailed. At that time, the British garrison in Kabul was forced to retreat. This first Anglo-Afghan War ended in a massacre of the British. Three years after British troops initialized their invasion, they withdrew through the Khyber Pass—a thirty-three-mile (fifty-three-kilometer) passage through the Hindu Kush that connects Afghanistan and Pakistan. Although legend stated that all but one man of the 16,500 people (4,500 soldiers and 12,000 camp followers) were killed while making their way out of the region, a handful of people survived. These men were actually taken as prisoners or hostages, but were later rescued by British troops that came in from Kandahar.

Dost Muhammad retook the throne in 1855, and over the next eight years, consolidated his power. He successfully unified Afghanistan, with the exception of Peshawar, before his death in 1863. Dost Muhammad's third son, Sher Ali, became emir of Afghanistan shortly after his father's death.

THE ILLUSTRATED LONDON NEWS

No. 2049.—VOL. LXXIII.   SATURDAY, OCTOBER 5, 1878.   WITH TWO SUPPLEMENTS. SIXPENCE. By Post, 6½d.

FORT OF ALI MUSJID, KHYBER PASS, WHERE THE BRITISH MISSION TO CABUL WAS TURNED BACK.

A. *Cantonment*
B. *Mission Residence*
C. *D° Offices*
D. *Magazine Fort (unfinished)*
E. *Commissariat Fort*
F. *Mahomed Shereef's Fort*
G. *Arkabashee Fort*
H. *Mahmood Khan's Fort*
I. *Zoolficar's Fort*
J. *Camp at Seeah Sung*
K. *King's Garden*
L. *Musjeed*
M. *Village of Behmaroo*
N. *Private Garden*
O. *Bazar*
P. *Kohistan Gate of City*
Q. *Empty Fort near Bridge*
R. *Brig.ʳ Anquetil's Fort*
S. *Magazine in Orchard*
T. *Yaboo khanch*
V. *Capt.ⁿ Trevor's Tower*
W. *Sir A. Burnes House*
X. *Lahore Gate of City*
Y. *Ruins of Serg.ᵗ Deane's House*
Z. *Capt.ⁿ Johnson's Treasury*

* *Denotes the spot where the Envoy was murdered.*

The second Anglo-Afghan War began in 1878 when British invaders advanced from India into Afghanistan. This conflict developed when Sher Ali allowed a Russian delegation

Both Britain and Russia used Afghanistan to protect their interests in northern India just as the country was beginning to assert its independence under Ahmad Shah. Russia attempted to persuade Persians to invade Afghanistan from the east in 1838, but they were counter-threatened by British forces, who instead invaded Afghanistan in 1839. This map illustrates the British cantonment, or troop quarters, during the first Anglo-Afghan War in Kabul. It wasn't long before Britain realized the force of the Afghan tribes and that its hope of protecting its interests in India would come more easily with Afghanistan on its side. Still, infighting between Afghan tribes led to vast civil unrest and killing in the streets. The *Illustrated London News (left)* often covered the conflict for Britain. British forces left Afghanistan by January 1842.

into Kabul but refused the same entrance to British delegates. One year later Sher Ali died. Before assuming his father's throne, Sher Ali's son Yaqub signed the Treaty of Gandamak, allowing the British in India to dictate Afghanistan's foreign affairs. After an uprising, however, Yaqub stepped down and the British and Russians agreed to have his half-cousin Abdur Rahman take over Kabul in 1880. Rahman's first task was to build Afghanistan into a unified and recognized central Asian power, finally forming the boundaries that now shape modern Afghanistan.

The Durand Line of 1893, drawn by the British, defined Afghanistan's easternmost border with British India. The border also established Afghanistan as a buffer between the Russian and British-Indian frontiers.

This colored engraving illustrates the retreat of British forces from Afghanistan in 1842. Thousands of British reportedly died in Afghanistan before the entire British army could assemble to leave the region. To this day, the first Anglo-Afghan War is considered the worst disaster in the history of the British military.

Dost Muhammad Khan (*left*) is often remembered as a diplomatic Afghan leader in an uncivilized time. While ruling the country from 1826 to 1863, he helped guide Afghanistan through a delicate balancing act between stronger British and Russian antagonists. In an attempt to secure better relations with Britain he signed several "treaties of friendship" during his reign. His son and successor, Sher Ali, also known as Muhammad Akbar Khan, took over for his father after his death in 1863, and is shown in the engraving below. Ali led the rising against British forces in 1842 before their withdrawal.

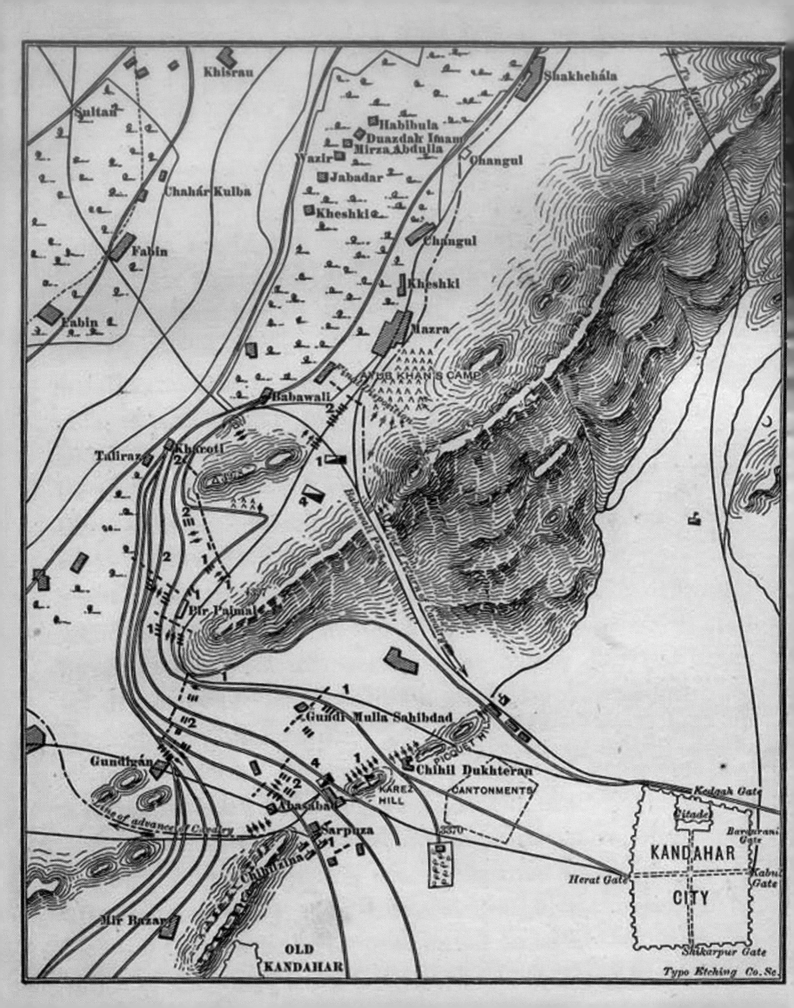

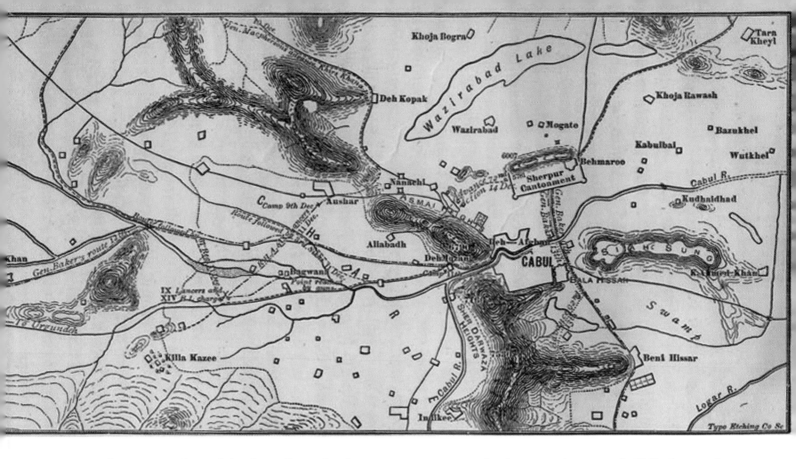

Unfortunately, this border designation split Afghan's tribal areas in half, leaving many of them, particularly the Pashtuns, in what is now Pakistan. Subsequent border decisions resulted from treaties between Russia and Britain, one that dated back to 1895, such as Afghanistan's northern border, and another in 1907, with its western neighbor, Iran.

It was also during this time that Afghanistan's northeastern "finger," known as the Wakhan Corridor, was established. This strip of isolated land borders Tajikistan in the north, the Xinjiang province of China in the east, and the regions of Gilgit and Chitral in Pakistan in the south.

Although as many as twenty small wars raged between Abdur Rahman Khan's rise to power and his death in 1901, he was able to preserve the independence of his newly formed country. Britain retained control, however, of all of Afghanistan's foreign affairs during his reign.

Abdur Rahman's son Habibullah continued in his father's footsteps of modernizing Afghanistan. Throughout his reign, Habibullah attempted to industrialize the country. He also helped it establish a

Both Kabul (*above*) and Kandahar (*left*) were invaded and then captured by British forces in the battles beginning the second Anglo-Afghan War (1878–1880), as illustrated in these maps, after a brief period of Afghan independence. Although Afghan leader Abdur Rahman rose to power after the fighting ceased, the Afghan government had little say in resolving its borders. During the 1880s, Russia formally occupied land north of the Amu Darya, which later become Afghanistan's northern (current) border.

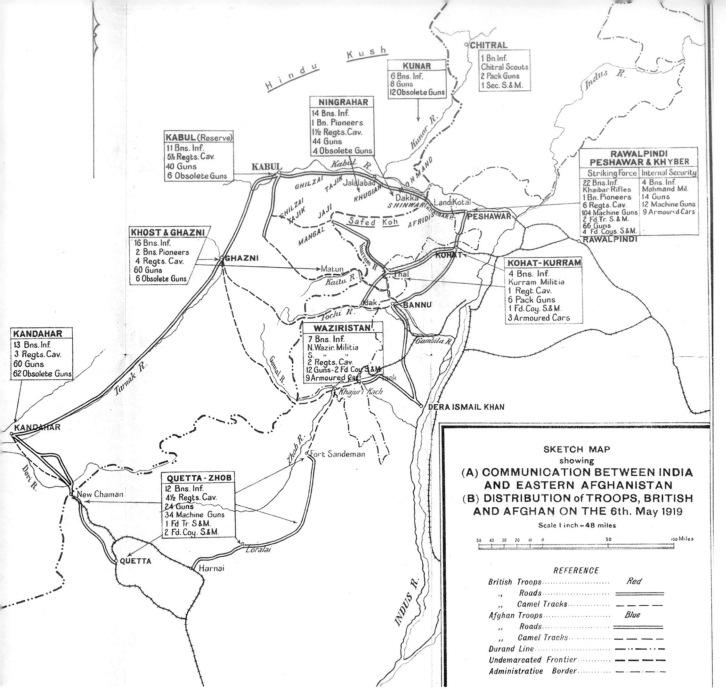

KABUL (Reserve)
11 Bns. Inf.
5½ Regts. Cav.
40 Guns
6 Obsolete Guns

NINGRAHAR
14 Bns. Inf.
1 Bn. Pioneers
1½ Regts. Cav.
44 Guns
4 Obsolete Guns

KUNAR
6 Bns. Inf.
8 Guns
12 Obsolete Guns

CHITRAL
1 Bn. Inf.
Chitral Scouts
2 Pack Guns
1 Sec. S.& M.

RAWALPINDI
PESHAWAR & KHYBER

Striking Force	Internal Security
22 Bns. Inf.	4 Bns. Inf.
Khaibar Rifles	Mohmand Mil.
1 Bn. Pioneers	14 Guns
6 Regts. Cav.	12 Machine Guns
104 Machine Guns	9 Armoured Cars
2 Fd. Tr. S.& M.	
66 Guns	
4 Fd. Coys. S.& M.	

KHOST & GHAZNI
16 Bns. Inf.
2 Bns. Pioneers
4 Regts. Cav.
60 Guns
6 Obsolete Guns

KOHAT-KURRAM
4 Bns. Inf.
Kurram Militia
1 Regt. Cav.
6 Pack Guns
1 Fd. Coy. S.& M.
3 Armoured Cars

KANDAHAR
13 Bns. Inf.
3 Regts. Cav.
60 Guns
62 Obsolete Guns

WAZIRISTAN
7 Bns. Inf.
N. Wazir. Militia
S. "   "
2 Regts. Cav.
12 Guns-2 Fd Coy S & M
9 Armoured Cars

QUETTA-ZHOB
12 Bns. Inf.
4½ Regts. Cav.
24 Guns
34 Machine Guns
1 Fd Tr S & M
2 Fd. Coy. S.& M.

SKETCH MAP
showing
(A) COMMUNICATION BETWEEN INDIA
AND EASTERN AFGHANISTAN
(B) DISTRIBUTION of TROOPS, BRITISH
AND AFGHAN ON THE 6th. May 1919

Scale 1 inch = 48 miles

REFERENCE

British Troops	Red
„ Roads	
„ Camel Tracks	
Afghan Troops	Blue
„ Roads	
„ Camel Tracks	
Durand Line	
Undemarcated Frontier	
Administrative Border	

This historic map from 1919 illustrates Afghanistan's southern and eastern boundaries, known as the Durand Line (1893). The border was named after a British administrator who decided its route along the natural range of the Hindu Kush. Today this same line separates Afghanistan from Pakistan in the south—a problematic border for years as it divided traditional tribal lands, leaving many Pashtuns in Pakistan.

system of modern education. After his death in 1919, his son and successor, Amanullah, instigated a brief war—the third Anglo-Afghan conflict, which effectively ended British control of Afghanistan's foreign affairs. The resulting 1921 agreement, called the Treaty of Rawalpindi, recognized Afghanistan as an independent nation. However, with complete independence from Great Britain came a swift cut in the country's subsidy (foreign support) money.

5 MODERNISM MEETS CONFLICT

Despite its internal and external independence, Afghanistan's forward momentum would be short-lived. Amanullah Khan wanted control of Pashtun territory across the Durand Line, but was quickly stopped. Neighboring governments were building their military forces in an effort to establish their own power bases. Instead, Amanullah turned his attention to strengthening the Afghan government.

After securing independence from Britain, Amanullah signed a treaty of friendship with the newly established Union of Soviet Socialist Republics (USSR).

Between 1919 and 1929, Amanullah instituted dramatic government reforms. He changed the ruling title from *emir* (prince) to *padshah* (king) and introduced Afghanistan's first constitution in 1923. Amanullah created legislative councils, a judicial system, and secular (nonreligious) codes of law. He changed the country's system of taxation and budgeting. He also instituted social reforms that included abolishing the female *purdah* (a face-concealing veil), opening coeducational schools, introducing Western attire, and establishing educational programs. Resentment toward Amanullah's drastic changes grew rapidly, causing various uprisings throughout Afghanistan's countryside. Because he had let the country's armies weaken, tensions that began in the

western territory spread rapidly. Afghanistan was again catapulted into civil war by 1928.

Afghanistan's civil war ended one year later with Amanullah abdicating his throne and leaving the country. After brief control by Tajik forces—a group of Afghan nationals from tribes bordering on, or once located within, Tajikistan—who instigated Amanullah's overthrow, Muhammad Nadir Shah was elected in 1930 by *Loya Jirgah*—or the "Great Assembly"—with representatives from every

Afghan tribe in the country. Nadir, a descendent of Dost Muhammad, was supported by both the Pashtun Afghans and the Tajiks.

Muhammad Nadir Shah strengthened the country's armies and instituted less rigorous social reforms. By 1931, he had established a new constitution, basing his administration on orthodox Islamic law. Afghanistan's economy improved. Nadir Shah kept the country's international relationships neutral. Despite their continued interest in the region,

Amanullah Khan (*opposite, left*), king of Afghanistan from 1919 to 1929, was known as the country's Reform King. He was forced into exile after providing education for women and allowing Afghans to adopt more Western styles of dress. He is most often remembered for statements such as "Tribal custom must not impose itself on the free will of the individual." This photograph was taken in 1930, after he fled Afghanistan to Turkey. King Nadir Shah (*above*) of Afghanistan (1883–1933) holds a review of his troops from horseback on the day of his coronation in 1930.

Great Britain and the USSR remained distant. Still in need of international allies and assistance, however, Nadir Shah sought support from Europe and the United States.

The Presumption of Peace

Power inside Afghanistan would soon shift again. Nadir Shah was assassinated in 1933, and his nineteen-year-old son Zahir Shah took his father's title. Power remained with Zahir for the next forty years, during which time Afghanistan enjoyed a relatively peaceful existence.

Zahir Shah's forty-year reign saw a great many internal improvements and successes. During World War II,

when the entire world was being drawn to either the Axis powers (Germany, Italy, and Japan) or the Allied powers against them, Zahir Shah maintained Afghanistan's neutrality. He declared an official language for Afghanistan, Pashtu, which encouraged unity and nationalism among the Afghan people. Social reform was also embraced as Zahir

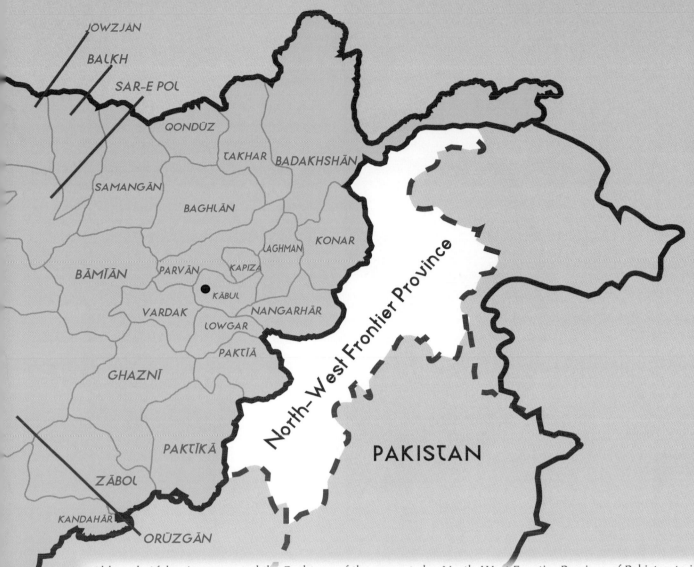

Although Afghanistan wanted the Pashtuns of the present-day North-West Frontier Province of Pakistan to join Afghanistan in 1947 when India became independent from Britain, they were not given that option. With their only available choice being to join either India or the newly formed country of Pakistan, the Pashtuns chose Pakistan, a decision that has since adversely affected relations between Afghanistan and Pakistan. Mohammad Zahir Shah (*pictured, bottom left*), king of Afghanistan from 1933 to 1973 and son of Nadir Shah, poses with his pet spaniel in 1950.

established the first university in Kabul. Economically, the founding of new textile industries, banking firms, and roadways were signs of progress. By 1946, Afghanistan was welcomed into the United Nations as it experienced its first democratic reforms.

In the fifty years since the Durand Agreement was signed, a steady anger grew over the splitting of the Pashtun tribes between Afghanistan and British India. In 1947, however, dissent erupted as India and Pakistan were created from the former British territory. Because Pashtun tribes were located primarily in Pakistan's North-West Frontier Province, Afghans argued that all Pashtuns should be given the opportunity to unite. Afghans wanted the Pashtun people to form an independent country instead of being forced to join either Pakistan or India. Since the creation of the proposed country (Pashtunistan) would destroy the newly named Pakistan, the Pakistani government reacted to the potential intrusion into their national status. Pakistan formally closed its borders with Afghanistan.

With vital trade routes through Pakistan to India closed, Afghanistan turned to the USSR for assistance. The Russians willingly purchased Afghanistan's annual harvest, saving the country from an instant economic crisis. King Zahir Shah appointed his cousin Mohammad Daoud as prime minister in 1953 to help initiate economic stimulation programs for Afghanistan. He hoped to offset the country's lost trade and reduce its financial dependence on the USSR.

Daoud was prime minister for ten years, often setting the United States and the Soviet Union against each other in order to gain economic support for his struggling country. To his credit, he was responsible for very progressive reforms. He had a pro-Pashunistan platform, however, and during his tenure as prime minister, relations with Pakistan worsened. In 1963, Daoud was forced to resign. Tensions with Pakistan eased, and the borders were reopened. But Daoud's impact on Afghanistan's history was not over.

It was also during the political democratic experiments of the 1960s that the growth of Afghanistan's political parties developed. The most notable organization was the People's Democratic Party of Afghanistan (PDPA). Also called the Afghan Communist Party, the PDPA had close ideological ties to Russia.

In 1967, the PDPA was divided into two factions—Khalq (Masses) and Parcham (Banner). Khalq followers had an allegiance to the GRU, a secret military unit within the

Mohammed Daoud, first prime minister (1953 to 1963), then president (1973 to 1978) of Afghanistan, was shot and killed by rebel troops when he refused to surrender during a coup. This photograph was taken shortly before the forced overthrow of his administration on April 28, 1978.

Russian government. The Khalq faction, led by Nur Muhammad Taraki, was very well organized. It was largely composed of Afghanistan's "common man." The Parcham faction had an allegiance to Russia's KGB, the secret police, and were considered urban intellectuals. They were led by Babrak Karmal, had a diversity of backgrounds, and were generally considered unorganized. The two factions represented the deep ethnic, class, and ideological divisions within Afghanistan's society.

The reforms were unsuccessful, and political instability and economic conditions worsened. Additionally, Zahir Shah's government realized that Afghanistan's new constitutional terms, which allowed for elected officials, free speech, and social reforms, opened the way for critical examination by Afghan citizens. By 1962, the government had abandoned its belief in these democratic philosophies and assumed a control that more closely resembled a monarchy. Afghans had already learned of the new tools of opposition in a democratic environment, however, and did not wish to retreat to the tighter restrictions.

The Formation of a Republic

While Afghanistan's government struggled to control its people, a new force was rising on its eastern border.

For another decade Zahir Shah experimented with constitutional changes in Afghanistan. He instituted its transition from an absolute to a constitutional monarchy and introduced a variety of election formats and economic programs. Despite Zahir Shah's progressive acts, Afghanistan's tense political position was worsened by severe droughts in 1971 and 1972. The country faced enormous loss of life and income. In 1973, Zahir Shah still failed to guide Afghanistan to economic recovery. On July 17, 1973, Afghanistan entered a new era.

In a coup orchestrated while Zahir Shah was out of the country, Mohammad Daoud returned to Afghanistan's political landscape. He seized power from the king with support from officers of the Parcham faction trained in the USSR. He then abolished the constitution and declared Afghanistan a republic, naming himself its prime minister and first president.

6 THE SOVIET OCCUPATION

Daoud's republic struggled for five years against charges of corruption and economic failure. Unfortunately, his attempts to reform Afghanistan collapsed.

In April 1978, the reunified PDPA, with Moscow's support, initiated a coup that resulted in the overthrow of Daoud's administration as well as his death. This overthrow was known as the Saur (April) Revolution. Nur Muhammad Taraki, formerly secretary general of the PDPA, became president of the Revolutionary Council and president of the newly established Democratic Republic of Afghanistan.

The Strengthening Soviet Foothold

With PDPA rule, chaos and confusion dominated the Republic of Afghanistan. The brutal Soviet style of the PDPA's politics was dramatically opposed to

By 1978, Afghanistan was growing increasingly unstable. General Daoud was overthrown as its president and killed by a leftist member of the People's Democratic Party of Afghanistan (PDPA). More conservative factions of the PDPA that objected to Afghanistan's growing social changes also began to gain power at this time, and revolts became commonplace throughout the Afghan countryside. Once the Afghan army faced certain collapse, the Soviet Union sent in troops backing PDPA Parcham faction leader Babrak Karmal.

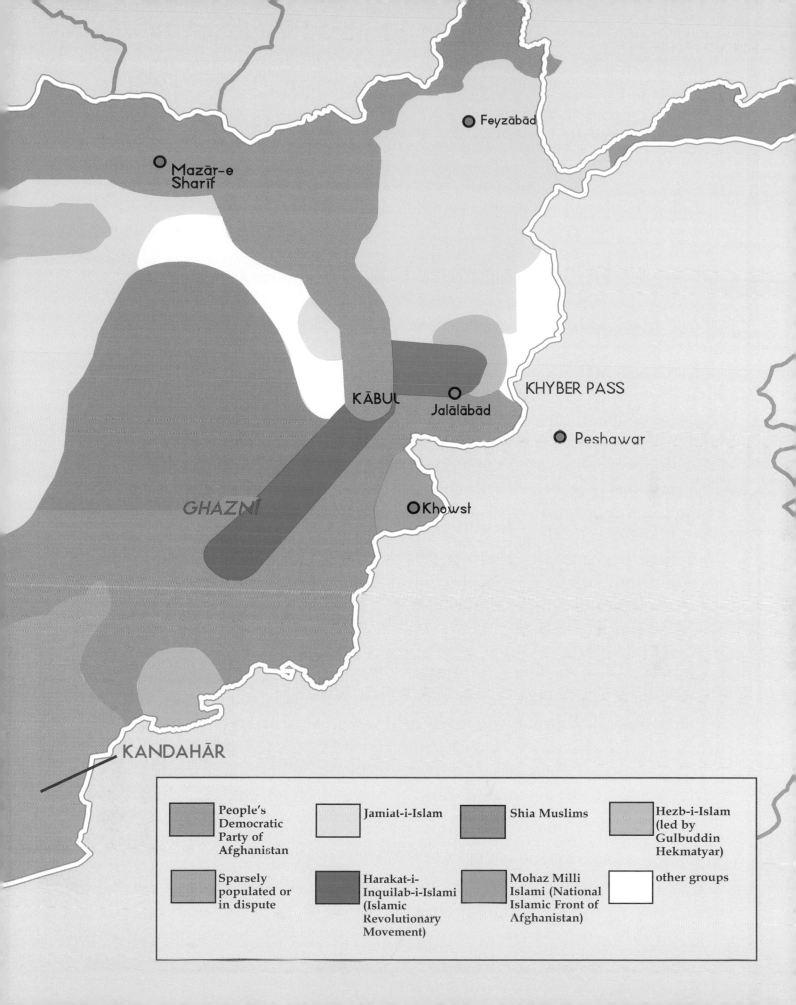

Feyzābād

Mazār-e
Sharīf

KĀBUL

KHYBER PASS

Jalālābād

Peshawar

GHAZNĪ

Khowst

KANDAHĀR

People's
Democratic
Party of
Afghanistan

Jamiat-i-Islam

Shia Muslims

Hezb-i-Islam
(led by
Gulbuddin
Hekmatyar)

Sparsely
populated or
in dispute

Harakat-i-
Inquilab-i-Islami
(Islamic
Revolutionary
Movement)

Mohaz Milli
Islami (National
Islamic Front of
Afghanistan)

other groups

Afghanistan's deeply rooted Islamic traditions. By 1979, a second revolution ousted Taraki's government. A new regime that relied even more heavily on Soviet support was installed in its place. A year later, Taraki's successor, Hafizullah Amin, would face a similar fate as the Soviets became increasingly frustrated with his refusal to make changes to stabilize the Afghan government.

Moscow's military presence began in 1978 when Afghanistan signed a treaty of cooperation with the Soviet Union. This agreement provided military aid in situations that threatened governmental power. As uprisings became common, additional military support was required in Afghanistan. Soviet forces were spending an increasing amount of time within the war-torn country. Large numbers of Soviet air forces joined ground troops in Kabul in 1979 under the pretext of routine exercises. Weeks later, these forces killed Hafizullah Amin and installed Babrak Karmal, the former head of the Parcham faction of the PDPA, as prime minister. Massive Soviet forces then descended from the north.

Following the Soviet invasions of 1979, and despite some 120,000 Soviet troops that remained to protect the new Karmal regime, Afghanistan's countryside remained chaotic.

Afghans generally opposed the Communist presence, and freedom fighters known as *mujahideen* made it impossible for Karmal to maintain a system of government. Poorly armed and organized at first, by 1984 the mujahideen had received substantial assistance in the form of weapons and training from the United States.

Now armed, the mujahideen took a more aggressive stance against the Soviet invaders, and an Islamic holy war (*jihad*) was declared. Two unified groups of muhajideen were formed. In 1985, seven Peshawar-based Sunni Muslim guerrilla organizations joined forces, calling themselves the Islamic Union of Afghan Mujahideen. Two years later, eight Shiite Afghan groups from Iran banded together to form the Islamic Coalition Council of Afghanistan.

Although the Soviet-installed Karmal government tried to control the country and attack the guerrillas, mujahideen forces assassinated government officials and attacked buildings. The Karmal regime was forcibly removed in 1986 amid great Soviet displeasure, and a former chief of the Afghan secret police, Muhammad Najibullah, was installed as prime minister. In 1987, Najibullah was elected president. He never won international recognition, territorial control, or popular support, yet his presidency continued until 1992.

A Temporary Resolution

The Soviet occupation of Afghanistan went poorly, and talk of withdrawal began as early as 1982. By the mid-1980s, the United States, Pakistan, Saudi Arabia, and others backed Afghanistan's resistance. The USSR's military losses were great—estimated to be nearly 50,000—and Russia's relations with Western and Islamic powers were suffering. Finally, in 1988, the Pakistani and Afghan governments, supported by both the USSR and the United States, signed an agreement settlement. The five documents of this agreement were known as the Geneva Accords.

This agreement called for Soviet and U.S. noninterference in Afghan-Pakistani affairs, the right of refugees to return to Afghanistan without fear of persecution, and the total withdrawal of Soviet troops from Afghanistan by February 15, 1989.

Although the talks were considered successful, the mujahideen, who were not asked to take part in the

Rebels advanced on Jalalabad in February 1989, when the National Islamic Federation of Afghanistan (NIFA) took a fifteen-mile (twenty-five-kilometer) stretch of the Kabul/Jalalabad Road. The city of Jalalabad was cut off from the Afghan government completely, a crushing defeat for the administration. Commander Shahrukh Grah, a man who previously worked as a doctor in Kabul, led the attack.

conferences, did not accept these terms. The Soviets withdrew their troops according to the guidelines, but the civil war continued. With the mujahideen leading the way, Afghanistan's conflicts escalated. Tribal infighting continued in Afghanistan, and the United States and Soviet Union supplied money and weapons to the rebels for three more years. In 1992, Najibullah and his armies were permanently removed from Kabul. The mujahideen coalition was victorious. Afghanistan's city of Kabul was now under the leadership of Tajik commander Ahmad Shah Massoud.

Between 1992 and 1994, control over Kabul and the government floundered. Gulbuddin Hekmatyar, the Pashtun leader of the fundamentalist Hezb-i-Islam mujahideen forces, had his own plans for Afghanistan. He wanted to apply strict Islamic law, while Massoud favored moderation.

The coalition arranged for the appointment of Sibgatullah Mohaddedi to the position of chair of the Islamic Jihad Council. Within a year, Mohaddedi turned his presidency over to Burhanuddin Rabbani, a political leader of the Jamiat-i-Islami, or Society of Islam Party. Massoud was the military leader of that party. His appointment placed the majority of the power with Afghanistan's Tajik minority—about one-fourth of the

Commandant Ahmad Shah Massoud, legendary leader of Afghanistan's Northern Alliance, is seen here in a shelter in Afghanistan's Panjshir Valley region that was built by resisters trying to escape Soviet aggression in June 1985. Massoud was killed in 2001 in a suicide attack by members of the Islamic fundamentalist group Al Qaeda.

Afghan population. Because of this inequity, Hekmatyar refused to participate in the new government.

During the fourteen-year civil war that began with Soviet withdrawal from Afghanistan in 1979, more than one million people died. Another five million people fled the country as refugees. Afghanistan lost nearly 50 percent of its population and fighting also destroyed more than 100,000 acres of land.

7 THE RISE OF THE TALIBAN

The Rabbani government failed to end the tribal fighting in Afghanistan. Four separate peace agreements were reached, but each was short-lived.

Afghanistan was now divided into several independent zones. The civil war was escalating, and a militia of Pashtun Islamic fundamentalist students called the Taliban began to emerge. By 1994, they battled for their country's unification and became more powerful.

The Taliban emerged from religious schools in northwest Pakistan. In the early 1990s, the bulk of the Taliban came from Pakistan's Pashtun provinces. It was their goal to turn Afghanistan into a united state. The Taliban movement at that time represented the return of madrasa-based (religious-based) Islamic principals to Afghanistan's political scene. The stated mission of the Taliban was to disarm the country's warring factions. They sought to impose their own strict view of Islamic law.

At this time, the Taliban forces included a group of Afghan refugees who had fled to Pakistan during previous invasions. Former rebel fighters and communist soldiers completed the Taliban's ranks.

The Government Changes Hands

Abdul Hakim Sharai was a leader in the Taliban movement in 1994. He was chief of security in the

southeastern province of Khost and had become governor of a neighboring province, Zobul. Under Sharai's direction, Taliban forces made effective military gains. With the use of armor, rocket artillery, and helicopters—all rumored to be largely funded by drug money—Taliban armies captured Kandahar in November 1994. By 1995, they also controlled the Ghazni province northeast of Kandahar, and they spent the next nine months strengthening their hold over southern Afghanistan. Eight months later, Taliban forces captured Herat in the west. By 1996, they had seized Kabul and gained control of the country.

With the Taliban conquest of Kabul, Burhanuddin Rabbani's reign came to an abrupt end. The Rabbani government had formally expired in 1994, but due to the intensity of the civil war he had retained his office. In an effort to prevent further Taliban advances, Rabbani welcomed Gulbuddin Hekmatyar, his onetime opponent and former prime minister, back into this post. The alliance proved to be too late, however, and Rabbani's government was forced to retreat to the northeastern provinces shortly after Kabul fell. The Taliban government formally changed the country's name to the Islamic Emirate (State) of Afghanistan, which remains official to this day.

Rabbani and Hekmatyar aligned themselves with other anti-Taliban factions, taking the name United Islamic Front for the Salvation of Afghanistan (UNIFSA), most commonly referred to as the Northern Alliance. Northern Alliance forces were centered in the Panjshir Valley located at the western edge of the Hindu Kush, north of Kabul, and were estimated to number approximately 15,000.

Although the Taliban continued northward, their advance was temporary. They were defeated by the Northern Alliance in 1997.

Al Qaeda

With the Taliban came the defeat of communism within Afghanistan and the notion of a unified nation. Nearly 40 percent of the country traced its ancestry to Pashtun families, and almost 85 percent of Afghanistan's population is Sunni Muslim, as are the Taliban. Some

In the 1990s Afghanistan's potential for ongoing problems swelled into a fury as the Taliban gained power with their ultraconservative form of Islamic fundamentalism. Little by little, however, all surrounding countries, including once-supportive nations such as Pakistan—which is also a Muslim country—were alienated from the war-torn and isolated region.

Taliban forces, like the rebels pictured in this photo, reached the height of their power when they captured Kabul in September 1996 and installed a strict Islamic regime in Afghanistan. With the aim of outlawing any outside influences that would oppose their fundamentalist viewpoint, Afghanistan continually struggled with a wealth of ongoing issues such as poor public health, famine, increased poverty, few human rights and freedoms, a breakdown in education, and the continuous growth of displaced citizens.

people believed in supporting the Taliban government to restore unity to the war-torn nation.

Unfortunately, the Taliban focused largely on persuading the Afghan people to subscribe to their puritanical Islamic view rather than rebuilding the nation. Afghanistan was still plagued by famine, refugees, and a growing public health crisis. In the end, only three countries would recognize the Taliban as a legal government: Pakistan, Saudi Arabia, and the United Arab Emirates.

Saudi Arabia's support of the Taliban was unexpected. In addition to conflicting with their strict interpretation of Sunni Muslim laws, the Saudi government had accused Afghanistan of harboring Saudi dissident Osama bin Laden. The goal of bin Laden's Al Qaeda is to unite all Muslims under one strict Islamic government. Al Qaeda members believe that the United States is an enemy of Islam. After a brief period of exile in the Sudan, bin Laden moved to Afghanistan in 1996. He and his Al Qaeda fighters are presumed to have remained there, under the protection of the Taliban.

The Tie to Terrorism

In 1998, while the Taliban was attempting to capture Afghanistan's northern territories, its Saudi ally bin Laden was making movements of his own. Two U.S. Embassies—one in Kenya and the other in Tanzania—were bombed. Two hundred people were killed, and another 4,500 injured. Bin Laden and his Al Qaeda network were suspected of these terrorist attacks.

Osama bin Laden

Osama bin Laden, a multimillionaire born to a wealthy family in Riyadh, Saudi Arabia, was expelled from his home country in 1991. His Saudi citizenship was revoked in 1994 because of his political activities. These antigovernment actions were founded in bin Laden's displeasure with Saudi Arabia's alliance with the United States during the Persian Gulf War (1990–1991).

Bin Laden studied civil engineering at the King Abdul Aziz University in Jeddah on the eastern shore of the Red Sea. He joined Afghanistan's mujahideen in the fight against the Soviets in 1979. Still in Pakistan in the late 1980s, bin Laden founded an organization of Muslim fighters known as Al Qaeda.

Meanwhile, the Taliban advanced to Mazar-e-Sharif and Bamiyan in the central region of Hazarajat. The Taliban, allegedly at the cost of some 8,000 Afghan lives, took control of nearly 90 percent of Afghanistan.

Under the leadership of Mullah Muhammad Omar, and with the support of bin Laden's millions, the Taliban became even more powerful. To many, their success is due in large part to the open support of General Pervez Musharaf and Pakistan's government. Some experts theorize that Pakistan supported the Taliban only to ensure constant infighting and Pakistani influence in Afghan affairs. According to this assumption,

Pakistan wanted the conflicts kept out of the North-West Frontier Province of Pakistan.

The War on Terrorism

The United States was involved in Afghan politics since the Soviet occupation. The U.S. aid to the anti-Soviet forces unintentionally laid the foundation for the rise of the Taliban and other Islamic militant groups.

In response to the 1998 terrorist bombings at the U.S. Embassies in Kenya and Tanzania, the United States launched a devastating military assault on terrorist training camps in eastern Afghanistan. In retaliation, Taliban forces killed a United Nations official. This violence led UN aid agencies to temporarily halt desperately needed food and medical supplies from reaching Afghan refugees.

With increasing tensions between the United States and the Taliban, they each agreed to meet in Turkmenistan in 1998 for peace talks. The resulting agreement to share power was short-lived, however, and a second round of talks in Tashkent, Uzbekistan, failed to produce even a temporary accord.

Still searching for someone to hold accountable for the embassy bombings, the United States accused the Taliban of protecting bin Laden

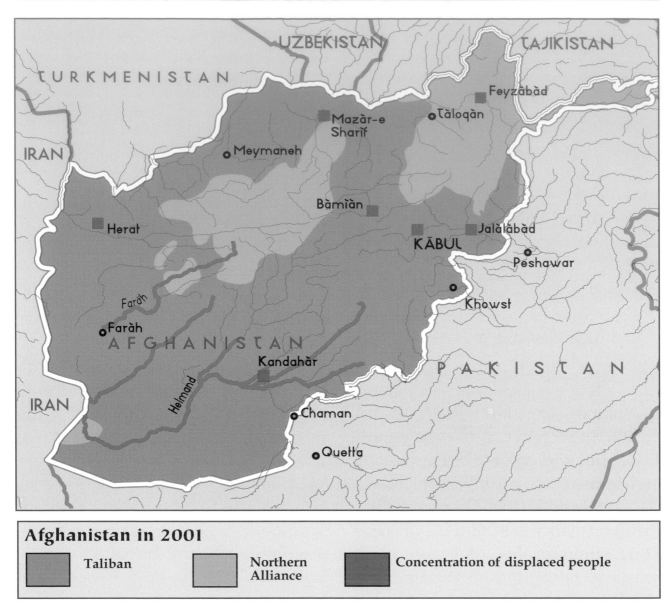

Afghanistan in 2001

	Taliban		Northern Alliance		Concentration of displaced people

This map, which shows the concentration of Taliban and Northern Alliance forces, as well as displaced Afghan refugees prior to October 2001, is but one example of the destruction of the country and its people. Figures from the time estimate that more than 3.5 million Afghans had been driven from their homes by war, hunger, and fear. While some fled to neighboring Pakistan, others crossed the border into Iran. Recently tabulated statistics claim that about 1.2 million Afghans live as nomads in tent shelters and mud huts in Pakistan, while 1.5 million live in Iran.

and demanded his surrender. In 1999, after receiving acknowledgments that bin Laden was, in fact, under Taliban protection, the UN imposed severe economic sanctions against Afghanistan.

At this time the Northern Alliance commander, Ahmad Shah Massoud, was believed to be the only man who could unite the different Afghan factions into a single anti-Taliban force. Since 1994, Russia, Tajikistan, Iran,

India, and the United States have all funded Northern Alliance efforts.

In September 2001, however, suspected Taliban militia assassinated Massoud. Although Burhanuddin Rabbani remained the political leader of the United Islamic Front for the Salvation of Afghanistan, Muhammad Fahim was named as his successor. He is still the recognized leader of the Northern Alliance.

The Americans Take Action

Two days after Massoud's assassination, terrorists hijacked three passenger planes from airports in Boston, Massachusetts, and Washington, D.C. They then proceeded to deliberately crash them into the twin towers of the World Trade Center in New York City and the Pentagon outside of Washington, D.C. A fourth plane was also hijacked, and as a result of the efforts of passengers and crew, it crashed into a field in central Pennsylvania. It was widely accepted that the Taliban, bin Laden, and the Al Qaeda network were behind these attacks. More than 3,000 people were killed.

Following those attacks, Afghanistan was again in the international spotlight. The United States accused the Taliban of protecting bin Laden and demanded that he be turned over to United Nations authorities. When the Taliban refused to shut down its camps and hand over bin Laden, the United States and its allies launched a military campaign against them. Afghanistan fell victim to massive air strikes as well as a ground offensive designed to destroy Taliban power. Operation Enduring Freedom, as the offensive was called, was successful in achieving this short-term goal, and the Taliban was removed from power by December 2001. The U.S. forces, however, remain in Afghanistan.

A New Government

With the removal of the Taliban, Afghanistan announced the establishment of a temporary government, which assumed power in Kabul in 2001. It comprised leaders of Tajik, Pashtun, and Hazara Afghans and included a chairman, five deputies a twenty-one-member Loya Jirgah, a Supreme Court, and a security force. At the time of this writing, Afghan officials nominated Hamed Karzai as the new head of Afghanistan for eighteen months beginning in June 2002.

TIMELINE

5000 BC Mesopotamia flourishes

3300 BC Writing begins in Sumer

2500 BC Egyptians build the Pyramids

2400 BC Assyrian Empire is established

2334 BC Rule of Sargon I

1750 BC Rule of Hammurabi in Babylonia

638 BC Approximate birth of Persian prophet Zoroaster (Zarathrustra)

600 BC Cyrus the Great establishes the Achaemenid Empire

563 BC Approximate birth of Buddha

331 BC Alexander the Great captures Babylon

323 BC Alexander the Great dies

AD 200 Sassanians rise to power

AD 226 Approximate date Zoroastrianism is established

AD 313 Christianity is accepted by the Romans

AD 570 Birth of Muhammad

AD 600 Roman, Parthian, and Kushan Empires flourish

AD 610 Muhammad's first revelation

AD 622 Buddhism begins its spread from India to Asia

AD 625 Muslims control Mesopotamia and Persia

AD 632 Death of Muhammad

AD 633–700 Followers of Islam start to spread their faith

AD 685 Shiite revolt in Iraq

AD 750 Abbasid caliphate, Iraq

AD 751 Arabs learn papermaking from the Chinese

AD 762 City of Baghdad is founded

AD 1215 Genghis Khan captures China and moves westward

AD 1220 Mongols sack Bukhara, Samarkand, and Tashkent

AD 1258 Mongols sack Baghdad

AD 1379 Timur invades Iraq

AD 1387 Timur conquers Persia

AD 1453 Ottoman Empire captures Constantinople and begins overtaking Asia

AD 1498 Vasco da Gama reaches India

AD 1526 Babur establishes Mughal Empire

AD 1534 Ottomans seize Iraq

AD 1554 First Russian invasion into central Asia

AD 1632 Taj Mahal is built

AD 1739 Nadir Shah invades the Mughal Empire, sacks Delhi,

AD 1740 Ahmad Shah Durrani founds kingdom in Afghanistan

AD 1858 British rule is established in India

AD 1932 Saudi Arabia is founded by 'Abd al-'Aziz Al Sa'ud

AD 1947 India declares its independence; East/West Pakistan succession

AD 2001 Ahmed Shah Amsood killed by assassins posing as journalists

AD 2001 U.S. begins military strikes in Afghanistan after September 11 attacks

AD 2001 Hamed Karzai becomes new leader of Afghanistan

AD 2002 Former king Zahir returns to Afghanistan but lays no claim to title

GLOSSARY

Achaemenid The ruling dynasty of Persia established by Cyrus the Great and lasting until the death of Darius III (533–330 BC).

Alexander the Great The king of Macedonia; conqueror of Greece, the Persian Empire, and Egypt.

Amu Darya A river in central Asia forming part of Afghanistan's northern border on its course.

Babur (also Babar, Baber) A Mughal conqueror of India (1483–1530). His original name was Zuhir-ud-Din Muhammad.

Bactria (Balkh) An ancient kingdom of southwestern Asia, now a district of northern Afghanistan known as Balkh.

Buddhism Religion based on the teachings of Siddharta Gautama, the Buddha, that is common in eastern and central Asia.

Durand Line A boundary imposed by the British in 1893 that separated Afghanistan from British India.

Ghazni A city and commercial center of east-central Afghanistan; the capital of a former Muslim kingdom.

Indus A river originating in southwestern Tibet that flows through India and Pakistan.

Iran Formerly Persia. A country of southwestern Asia.

Islam A religion based upon the teachings of the prophet Muhammad and the belief in one god (Allah).

jihad An Islamic holy war; a struggle in defense of or to propagate Islam.

jirgah A Pashtun tribal assembly for decision making; literally, "circle."

Kabul The capital of Afghanistan in the east-central part of the country.

Khalq One of the two main factions of the People's Democratic Party of Afghanistan (PDPA); literally, "people" or "masses."

Loya Jirgah Great Council; highest representative institution in the Afghan state.

Macedonia Ancient kingdom, north of Greece, that reached the height of its power under Alexander the Great.

monarch A sole and absolute ruler of a state.

Mongol A member of one of the nomadic tribes of Mongolia.

Mughal Empire Dynasty founded by Turko-Mongol invader Babur in the 1500s that lasted 300 years.

Northern Alliance Anti-Taliban military alliance formally know as the United Islamic Front for the Salvation of Afghanistan.

Parcham One of the two main factions of the People's Democratic Party of Afghanistan; literally, "flag" or "banner."

PDPA People's Democratic Party of Afghanistan. The Afghan Communist party founded in 1965 with the goal of turning the feudal society into a socialist state.

Shia Muslim sect that holds that leadership of the Islamic community should be by dynastic succession from the prophet Muhammad and his descendents.

Sunni Muslim sect that holds that Muhammad's successor should be elected.

Taliban Religious students; literally, "seekers." The Taliban are a Pashtun-based armed political group that came to power in 1994.

terrorism The use or threat of violence to create fear or alarm.

FOR MORE INFORMATION

Web Sites

Due to the changing nature of Internet links, the Rosen Publishing Group, Inc., has developed an online list of Web sites related to the subject of this book. This site is updated regularly. Please use this link to access the list:

http://www.rosenlinks.com/liha/afgh/

FOR FURTHER READING

Adamec, Ludwig W. *Dictionary of Afghan Wars, Revolutions and Insurgencies.* Boston, MA: Scarecrow Press, 1996.

Adamec, Ludwig W. *Historical Dictionary of Afghanistan.* Boston, MA: Scarecrow Press, 1997.

Ali, Sharifah Enayat. *Afghanistan.* Tarrytown, NY: Marshall Cavendish, 1995.

Cordovez, Diego, and Selig S. Harrison. *Out of Afghanistan: The Inside Story of the Soviet Withdrawal.* New York: Oxford University Press, 1995.

Corona, Laurel. *Afghanistan* (Modern Nations of the World). Chicago, IL: Gale/Lucent Books, 2002.

Evans, Martin. *Afghanistan: A Short History of Its People and Politics.* New York: HarperCollins, 2002.

Marsden, Peter. *The Taliban.* New York: St. Martin's, 1998.

Rubin, Barnett R. *The Fragmentation of Afghanistan: State Formation and Collapse in the International System.* New Haven, CT: Yale University Press, 1995.

BIBLIOGRAPHY

CIA—The World Factbook. "Afghanistan." Retrieved January 31, 2001 (http://www.odci.gov/cia/publications/factbook/geos/af.html).

Girardet, Edward, and Jonathan Walter. *Essential Field Guides to Humanitarian and Conflict Zones: Afghanistan.* Geneva, Switzerland: For ICHR by CROSSLINES Communications, Ltd., 1998.

Girardet, Edward. "Eyewitness Afghanistan." *National Geographic,* Vol. 200, No. 6, December 2001, pp. 130–137.

Gouttierre, Thomas E. "Afghanistan." *World Book Online Americas Edition.* Retrieved February 7, 2001 (http://wbol/wbPage/na/ar/co/006700).

Microsoft Encarta Online Encyclopedia 2001. "Genghis Khan." Retrieved February 15, 2001 (http://encarta.msn.com).

Shroder, John Ford, contributor. "Afghanistan." Microsoft Encarta Online Encyclopedia 2001. Retrieved February 7, 2001 (http://encarta.msn.com).

Worldtravelguide.net. "Afghanistan History & Government." Retrieved January 31, 2002 (http://www.wtg-online.com).

INDEX

About the Author

Amy Romano is the author of numerous magazine articles on a range of topics for both consumer and business-to-business publications. This is her first book. Amy currently lives in Connecticut with her husband, Don, and their children, Claudia, Sam, and Jack.

Photo Credits

Series Design and Layout

Tahara Hasan

Editor

Joann Jovinelly

Photo Research

Elizabeth Loving

4-30-03 ✓